# Rhythm Workbook

## Primer Level

For Piano, Electronic Keyboard or Organ

## by Wesley Schaum

## Foreword

This book is planned as a supplement to a **primer level** method book. It can be used by students of *all ages*, children, teenagers and adults. The purpose is to help develop an understanding and feeling for fundamental rhythms. It is recommended that his book be started during the first month's piano study.

Practical, step-by-step lessons present *recognition* of the rhythmic symbols *first* - followed by counting. These symbols are then correlated with rhythmic drills, various time signatures and measure construction. Included are explanations of basic rhythmic terminology such as note head, stem, beam, staff, measure, bar line, rest, etc.

This edition has completely new music engraving designed to improve the visual image of counting and rhythms based on suggestions submitted by Alfred Cahn of Milwaukee, Wisconsin.

**Other Schaum Workbooks:**

*Primer Level*
    Theory Workbook, Primer Level
    Keynote Speller, Primer Level

*Level One*
    Theory Workbook, Level One
    Keynote Speller, Level One
    Rhythm Workbook, Level One
    Christmas Story Note Speller
    Composer Note Speller

*Level Two*
    Theory Workbook, Level Two
    Rhythm Workbook, Level Two
    Easy Keyboard Harmony, Book 1
    Scale Speller

## Schaum Publications, Inc.

EXCLUSIVELY DISTRIBUTED BY

**HAL•LEONARD®**
CORPORATION

7777 W. BLUEMOUND RD. P.O. BOX 13819 MILWAUKEE, WI 53213

T0116720

02-21

# INDEX - PRIMER LEVEL

# INDEX - LEVEL ONE

# Lesson 1.   Quarter Notes and Half Notes

Name _____   Date _____   Score _____

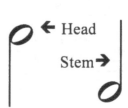

These are QUARTER Notes.
The round part of the note is called the HEAD.
*Notice that the note head is BLACK.*

The up-and-down line is called the STEM.
*Notice that the STEM may be placed above or below the note head.*

← Head
Stem →

**\*DIRECTIONS:**  Below are many different kinds of notes mixed together. Draw a circle around each QUARTER note. (You will find a total of *ten* Quarter Notes.)

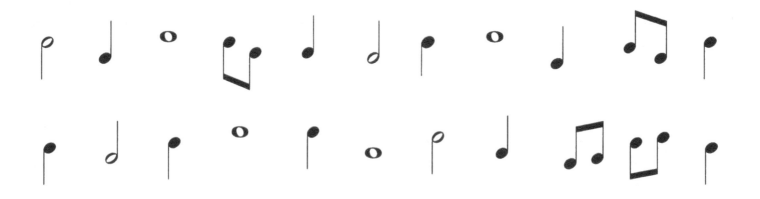

These are HALF notes.
*Notice that the note HEAD is WHITE inside.*
This is the only difference from a quarter note.

← Head
Stem →

**\*DIRECTIONS:**  Below are many different kinds of notes mixed together. Draw a circle around each HALF note. (You will find a total of *ten* Half Notes.)

**\*TEACHER'S NOTE:**  It is not intended that note values or counting be explained at this point. This will be done later. It is likewise not necessary to explain whole notes or eighth notes yet. Different kinds of notes are used to create a realistic sight-reading situation.

# Lesson 2.  Quarter Notes and Half Notes on the Staff

Name _____   Date _____   Score _____

This group of five lines is called the STAFF:

Notes may be placed *between* any staff
lines as shown below:

Any staff line may also go *through the
center* of a note head as shown below:

**\*DIRECTIONS:**  Draw a circle around all QUARTER notes on the staffs below.
(You will find *six* Quarter Notes on each staff.)

**DIRECTIONS:**  Draw a circle around all HALF notes on the staffs below.
(You will find *six* Half Notes on each staff.)

\*TEACHER'S NOTE:  Erasable ball-point pen or pencil may be used by the student.

# Lesson 3.  Identifying Quarter Notes and Half Notes

Name _____  Date _____  Score _____

**DIRECTIONS:** Write the letter "H" on the dotted line under each HALF note. Write the letter "Q" under each QUARTER note. If the note is *not* a Half or a Quarter note, do not write anything. (You will find four Half Notes and four Quarter Notes on each staff).

(sample)

H

(Write "H" for Half note; "Q" for Quarter note.)

(Write "H" for Half note; "Q" for Quarter note.)

# Lesson 4.  Quarter Note and Half Note Counting

Name _____   Date _____   Score _____

A QUARTER note gets ONE count.          A HALF note gets TWO counts.

$\quad$ = 1 Count                              $\quad$ = 2 Counts

**DIRECTIONS:**  Below are many different kinds of notes mixed together. Draw a circle around each ONE-COUNT note. (You will find *six* One-Count notes on each staff.)

**DIRECTIONS:**  Below are many different kinds of notes mixed together. Draw a circle around each TWO-COUNT note. (You will find *six* Two-Count notes on each staff.)

# Lesson 5.  Bar Lines and Measures

Name _____  Date _____  Score _____

Up-and-down lines on the staff are called BAR LINES.

BAR LINES

The section of the staff between bar lines is called a MEASURE.

←  MEASURE  →        ←  MEASURE  →        ←  MEASURE  →

**DIRECTIONS:**  Study the explanations above. Add up the One-Count and Two-Count notes and draw in *bar lines* as necessary to form measures. Each measure should have FOUR counts (see sample).

(sample)

(Draw in measure bar lines. Each measure should have *four* counts.)

(Reminder: Each measure should have *four* counts.)

# Lesson 6.   4/4 Time Signature and Counting

Name _____   Date _____   Score _____

The two large numbers on the staff are called a TIME SIGNATURE.

Time Signature
↓

4  ← Upper number means
      4 counts per measure.

4  ← Lower number means
      Quarter Note gets one count.

**DIRECTIONS:** Write in the counting on the dotted lines for every measure. Notice how the numbers in the sample measure are *evenly spaced*. See the back inside cover for additional samples of measure counting.

(sample)

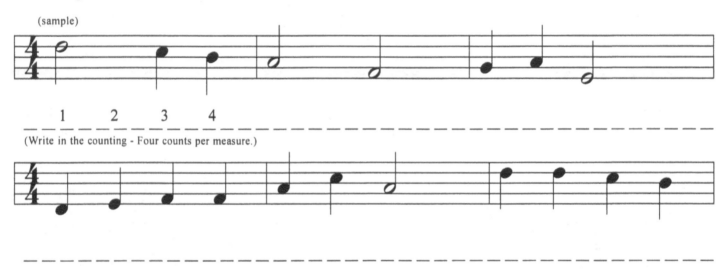

         1      2      3      4

(Write in the counting - Four counts per measure.)

**DIRECTIONS:** On the staffs below, the measure bar lines are missing. Write in the counting on the dotted lines. Then draw in bar lines where necessary to make *four counts* in each measure.

(Reminder: Write in the counting numbers *directly below* the note to which they apply.)

# Lesson 7. Changing Half Notes to Quarter Notes

Name _____  Date _____  Score _____

A HALF note may be changed to a QUARTER note, by coloring the note head BLACK.

**DIRECTIONS:** All the notes on the staffs below are half notes. Some of them will have to be changed to quarter notes to make FOUR COUNTS in each measure. Color note heads black where necessary. Then write in the counting on the dotted lines.

(sample)

1    2    3    4

(Change half notes to quarter notes where necessary, then write in the counting.)

(Reminder: Write in the counting numbers *directly below* the note to which they apply.)

**RHYTHM DRILL:** After writing in the counting for all the staffs above, *count aloud* "One-Two-Three-Four" to each measure and *clap hands* – one clap to each *note*. Also review lesson 6 in this way.

# Lesson 8.  Whole Notes

Name _____  Date _____  Score _____

This is a WHOLE note.

*Notice that it has NO STEM.*

**DIRECTIONS:** Below are many different kinds of notes mixed together. Draw a circle around each WHOLE note. (You will find *six* Whole Notes on each staff.)

**DIRECTIONS:** On the dotted lines under each of the notes on the following staffs, write the letter "W," "H" or "Q."

W = Whole Note        H = Half Note        Q = Quarter Note

(sample)

Q
_____

(Write "W" for Whole Note; "H" for Half Note; "Q" for Quarter Note.)

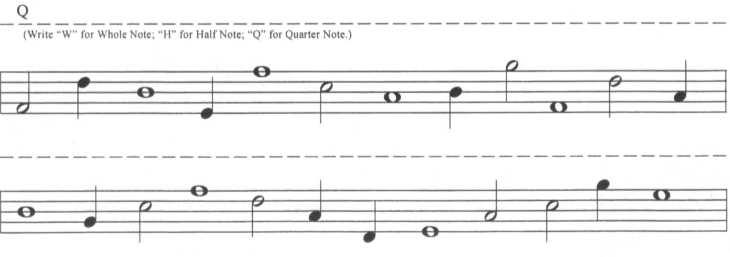

# Lesson 9. 4/4 Counting with Whole Notes

Name _____     Date _____     Score _____

A WHOLE note gets FOUR counts.

**O** = 4 counts          𝅗𝅥 = 2 counts          𝅘𝅥 = 1 count

**DIRECTIONS:** Write in the counting on the dotted lines for every measure. Notice how the numbers in the sample measure are *evenly spaced*. See the back inside cover for additional samples of measure counting.

(sample)

1   2   3   4
- - - - - - - - - - - - - - - - - - - - - - - - - - - - - - - - - - - - - - - - - - -

(Reminder: Write in the counting numbers *directly below* the note to which they apply.)

- - - - - - - - - - - - - - - - - - - - - - - - - - - - - - - - - - - - - - - - - - - -

- - - - - - - - - - - - - - - - - - - - - - - - - - - - - - - - - - - - - - - - - - - -

- - - - - - - - - - - - - - - - - - - - - - - - - - - - - - - - - - - - - - - - - - - -

- - - - - - - - - - - - - - - - - - - - - - - - - - - - - - - - - - - - - - - - - - - -

**RHYTHM DRILL:** After writing in the counting for the staffs above, *count aloud* "One-Two-Three-Four" to each measure and *clap hands* – one clap to each *note*.

# Lesson 10.  4/4 and "Common Time" Counting

Name _____  Date _____  Score _____

$\bigcirc$ = 4 counts      $\phantom{}$ = 2 counts      $\phantom{}$ = 1 count

**DIRECTIONS:** On the staffs below, the measure bar lines are missing. Write in the counting on the dotted lines. Then draw in the *bar lines* where necessary to make FOUR COUNTS in each measure.

(Write in the counting, then draw in the measure bar lines.)

**C** is the symbol for "Common Time."  It means the same as $\frac{4}{4}$ time.

(Write in the counting, then draw in the measure bar lines.)

**RHYTHM DRILL:** When finished, *count aloud and clap hands* (same as Lesson 9).

# Lesson 11. Placing Stems on Notes

Name _____  Date _____  Score _____

How to place STEMS on notes:

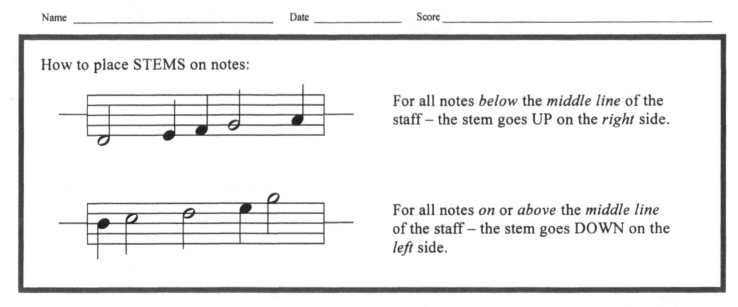

For all notes *below* the *middle line* of the staff – the stem goes UP on the *right* side.

For all notes *on* or *above* the *middle line* of the staff – the stem goes DOWN on the *left* side.

**DIRECTIONS:** Below is an assortment of note *heads* in various positions. Place a *stem* on each note head as explained at the top of this page.

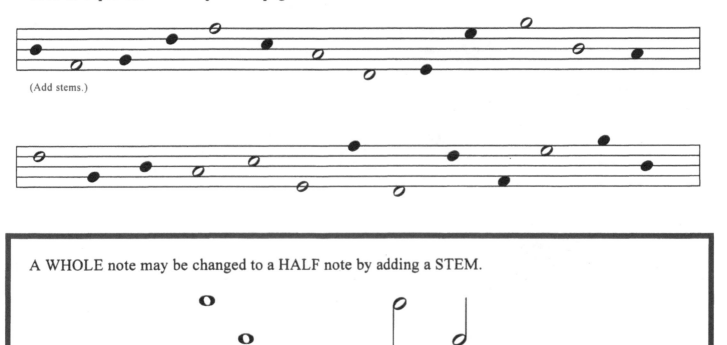

(Add stems.)

A WHOLE note may be changed to a HALF note by adding a STEM.

**DIRECTIONS:** Change all of the *whole* notes below to *half* notes by placing a *stem* on each note head.

(Change to half notes. Be careful of correct stem direction.)

# Lesson 12. Making Half and Quarter Notes

Name _____   Date _____   Score _____

A WHOLE note may be changed to a QUARTER note.

    1. By adding a stem to the note head

    2. By coloring the note head BLACK

**DIRECTIONS:** All of the notes below are *whole* notes. There should be FOUR COUNTS in each measure. Change some of the whole notes into *half* notes (see Lesson 11). Others will have to be changed to *quarter* notes (as described above). Then write in the counting on the dotted line below each measure (see sample).

(sample)   1      2      3      4

(Change into half notes or quarter notes to make *four counts* per measure.)

**RHYTHM DRILL:** When finished, *count aloud and clap hands* (same as Lesson 9).

# Lesson 13. Dotted Half Notes

Name _____  Date _____  Score _____

This is a DOTTED HALF NOTE.

It looks the same as a regular half note, except for the added dot.

**DIRECTIONS:** Below are many different kinds of notes mixed together. Draw a circle around each DOTTED HALF note. (You will find *five* Dotted Half Notes on each staff.)

**DIRECTIONS:** On the dotted lines under the notes on the following staffs, write the letter "W," "H," "DH" or "Q."

W = Whole Note          H = Half Note          DH = Dotted Half Note          Q = Quarter Note

(Write "W" for Whole note; "H" for Half note; "DH" for Dotted Half note; "Q" for Quarter note.)

# Lesson 14.  Dotted Half Note Counting

Name _____  Date _____  Score _____

A DOTTED HALF note gets THREE counts.

𝅗𝅥. = 3 counts

𝅝 = 4 counts          𝅗𝅥 = 2 counts          𝅘𝅥 = 1 count

**DIRECTIONS:** Write in the counting on the dotted lines for every measure. Notice how the numbers in the sample measure are *evenly spaced*. See the back inside cover for additional samples of measure counting.

(sample)

1    2    3    4

**DIRECTIONS:** The staffs below have missing measure bar lines. Write in the counting on the dotted lines below each note. Then draw in bar lines where necessary to make *four counts* in each measure.

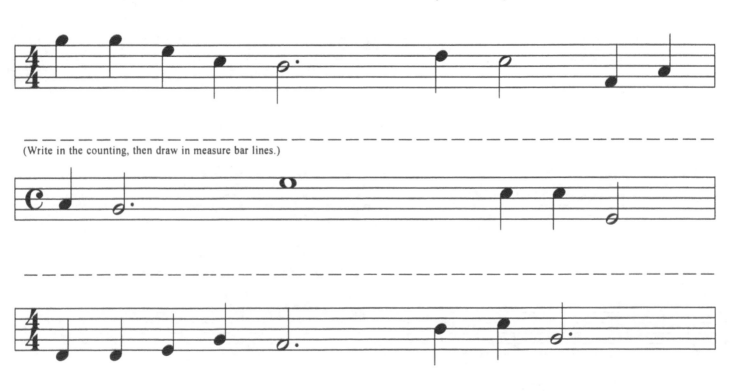

(Write in the counting, then draw in measure bar lines.)

**RHYTHM DRILL:** When finished, *count aloud and clap hands* (same as Lesson 9).

# Lesson 15. 3/4 Time Signature and Counting

Name _____ Date _____ Score _____

A NEW Time Signature:

$\frac{3}{4}$    →  Upper number means 3 counts per measure.

→  Lower number means Quarter note gets one count.

**DIRECTIONS:** Write in the counting on the dotted lines for every measure.

(sample)

_ _ 1 _ _ 2 _ _ 3 _ _ _ _ _ _ _ _ _ _ _ _ _ _ _ _ _ _ _ _ _ _ _ _ _ _ _ _ _ _ _ _ _

(Reminder: Write in the counting numbers *directly below* the note to which they apply.)

_ _ _ _ _ _ _ _ _ _ _ _ _ _ _ _ _ _ _ _ _ _ _ _ _ _ _ _ _ _ _ _ _ _ _ _ _ _ _ _ _

**DIRECTIONS:** On the staffs below, the measure bar lines are missing. Write in the counting on the dotted lines. Then draw in the bar lines where necessary to make *three counts* in each measure.

_ _ _ _ _ _ _ _ _ _ _ _ _ _ _ _ _ _ _ _ _ _ _ _ _ _ _ _ _ _ _ _ _ _ _ _ _ _ _ _ _

(Write in the counting, then draw in measure bar lines.)

_ _ _ _ _ _ _ _ _ _ _ _ _ _ _ _ _ _ _ _ _ _ _ _ _ _ _ _ _ _ _ _ _ _ _ _ _ _ _ _ _

_ _ _ _ _ _ _ _ _ _ _ _ _ _ _ _ _ _ _ _ _ _ _ _ _ _ _ _ _ _ _ _ _ _ _ _ _ _ _ _ _

**RHYTHM DRILL:** When finished, *count aloud and clap hands* (same as Lesson 9).

# Lesson 16. 2/4 Time Signature and Counting

Name _____ Date _____ Score _____

A NEW Time Signature:

$\frac{2}{4}$ ← Upper number means 2 counts per measure.

← Lower number means Quarter note gets one count.

 = 2 counts      = 1 count

**DIRECTIONS:** Write in the counting on the dotted lines for every measure.

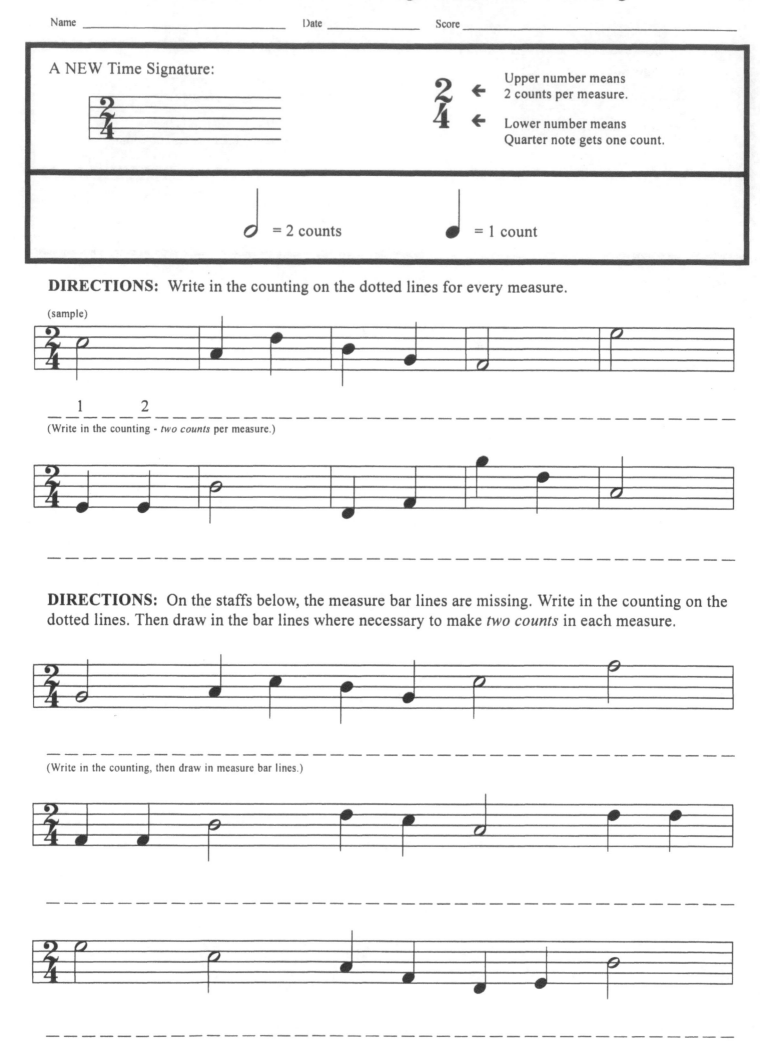

(sample)

____  1  ____  2  ____

(Write in the counting - *two counts* per measure.)

**DIRECTIONS:** On the staffs below, the measure bar lines are missing. Write in the counting on the dotted lines. Then draw in the bar lines where necessary to make *two counts* in each measure.

(Write in the counting, then draw in measure bar lines.)

**RHYTHM DRILL:** When finished, *count aloud and clap hands* (same as Lesson 9).

# Lesson 17. Various Time Signature Counting

Name _____ Date _____ Score _____

**DIRECTIONS:** Write in the counting for every measure. Be sure that the numbers are carefully placed *directly below* the note to which they apply. Watch for *different time signatures*.

(Write in the counting.)

(Reminder: Watch for *different* time signature.)

(Write in the counting.)

(Reminder: Watch for *different* time signature.)

(Write in the counting.)

**RHYTHM DRILL:** After writing in the counting for the staffs above, *count aloud* (according to the time signature) and *clap hands* – one clap to each note.

# Lesson 18.   Bar Line Placement with Various Time Signatures

Name _____   Date _____   Score _____

**DIRECTIONS:** On the staffs below, the measure bar lines are missing. Write in the counting on the dotted lines. Then draw in bar lines where necessary to fit with the time signature.

(Write in the counting, then draw in the measure bar lines.)

(Reminder: Watch for *different* time signature.)

(Reminder: Watch for *different* time signature.)

**RHYTHM DRILL:**  When finished, *count aloud and clap hands* (same as Lesson 17).

# Lesson 19.  Quarter and Half Rests

Name _____  Date _____  Score _____

This is a QUARTER REST.

Rests are signs of *silence*. They show places in music where *nothing* is to be played.
Rests are counted just the same as notes.

A quarter rest in the *staff* looks like this:

**DIRECTIONS:** Below are many different kinds of rests mixed together. Draw a circle around each QUARTER rest.

**DIRECTIONS:** Draw a circle around each QUARTER rest in the staff below. (You will find a total of *six* Quarter rests.)

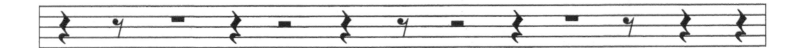

This is a HALF REST.

A half rest in the *staff* looks like this:

Notice that the *box-shaped* part of the half rest is *above* the middle staff line.

**DIRECTIONS:** Draw a circle around each HALF rest.

**DIRECTIONS:** Draw a circle around each HALF rest in the *staff* below. (You will find a total of *six* Half rests.)

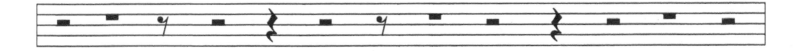

# Lesson 20.  Whole Rests

Name _____  Date _____  Score _____

---

This is a WHOLE REST.  ▬

A whole rest in the *staff* looks like this:

Notice that the *box-shaped* part of the whole rest is below the fourth staff line.

---

**DIRECTIONS:**  Below are many different kinds of rests mixed together. Draw a circle around each WHOLE rest.

**DIRECTIONS:**  Draw a circle around each WHOLE rest on the *staff* below. (You will find a total of *six* Whole rests.)

---

*Notice the difference: HALF and WHOLE rests.

The box-shaped part of a HALF rest is ABOVE the third staff line.

The box-shaped part of a WHOLE rest is BELOW the fourth staff line.

---

**DIRECTIONS:**  On the dotted lines under each of the rests on the following staffs, write the letter "W," "H" or "Q."

W = Whole Rest        H = Half Rest        Q = Quarter Rest

---

(Write "W" for Whole rest; "H" for Half rest; "Q" for Quarter rest.)

---

*TEACHER'S NOTE:  You may want to point out that a HALF rest is "lighter" and "floats on top" of the staff line. A WHOLE rest is "heavier" and "sinks below" the staff line.

# Lesson 21.  Counting Various Rests

Name _____    Date _____    Score _____

| | | |
|---|---|---|
| A WHOLE rest | ▬ | = 4 counts |
| A HALF rest | ▬ | = 2 counts |
| A QUARTER rest | 𝄾 | = 1 count |

**DIRECTIONS:**  Write in the counting for each measure. Be sure that the numbers are carefully placed *directly below* the rest to which they apply.

(sample)  1      2

(Write in the counting.)

(Reminder: Watch for *different* time signature.)

(Reminder: Watch for *different* time signature.)

# Lesson 22. Counting Various Notes and Rests Combined

Name _____    Date _____    Score _____

Rests are counted the same as notes.

    ▬ = 4 counts = 𝅝

    ▬ = 2 counts = 𝅗𝅥

    𝄽 = 1 count = 𝅘𝅥

**DIRECTIONS:** Write in the counting for each measure. Be sure that the numbers are carefully placed *directly below* the note or rest to which they apply.

(Write in the counting.)

(Reminder: Watch for *different* time signature.)

**RHYTHM DRILL:** After writing in the counting for the staffs above, *count aloud* for each measure (according to the time signature). *Clap hands* on the *notes*, but *be silent* for the *rests* by keeping hands apart for the duration of each rest.

# Lesson 23. Bar Line Placement with Rests and Notes

Name _____  Date _____  Score _____

**DIRECTIONS:** On the staffs below, the measure bar lines are missing. Write in the counting on the dotted lines. Then draw in bar lines where necessary to fit with the *time signature*.

(Write in the counting, then draw in the measure bar lines.)

(Reminder: Watch for *different* time signature.)

(Reminder: Write in the counting numbers *directly below* the note or rest to which they apply.)

**RHYTHM DRILL:** When finished, *count aloud and clap hands* (same as Lesson 22).

# Lesson 24.   Eighth Note Pairs

Name _____   Date _____   Score _____

These are EIGHTH notes.

When the stems of two quarter notes are joined by a heavy line called a BEAM, they become eighth notes.

Beam ↓

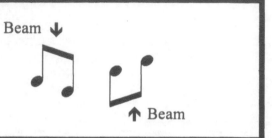

↑ Beam

**DIRECTIONS:** Draw a circle around each group of TWO EIGHTH NOTES.

**DIRECTIONS:** On the dotted line under the notes on the following staffs, write the letter "W," "H," "DH," "Q" or "E."

W = Whole         H = Half         DH = Dotted Half         Q = Quarter         E = Eighth

(Write "W" for Whole note; "H" for Half note; "DH" for Dotted Half note; "Q" for Quarter note; "E" for Eighth note.)

TEACHER'S NOTE:  Single eighth notes will be presented in a later book, along with dotted quarter notes.

# Lesson 25. One-Count Units

Name _____ Date _____ Score _____

Two EIGHTH notes together get ONE COUNT.

♫ = 1 count       ♩ = 1 count       𝄽 = 1 count

**DIRECTIONS:** Draw a circle around each ONE COUNT *note* and *rest* (including groups of *two eighth notes*).

(Circle each *one count* note and rest, including *eighth note* groups.)

# Lesson 26.  Eighth Note Counting

Name _____   Date _____   Score _____

*EIGHTH notes are counted like this:

1  +  2  +  3     4  +     1     2     3  +  4

**DIRECTIONS:** Write in the counting for each measure. Be sure that the numbers and abbreviations are carefully placed *directly below* the note or rest to which they apply.

(sample)

1  +  2     3     4

(Write in the counting.)

(Reminder: Watch for *different* time signatures.)

(Reminder: Write in the counting numbers *directly below* the note or rest to which they apply.)

*TEACHER'S NOTE: The plus sign is used as an abbreviation for "and." If you prefer, an "a" or an ampersand (&) could be used instead.

# Lesson 27. Counting and Bar Line Placement

Name _____ Date _____ Score _____

**DIRECTIONS:** On the staffs below, the measure bar lines are missing. Write in the counting on the dotted lines. Then draw in the bar lines where necessary (watch for *different time signatures*).

(Write in the counting, then draw in measure bar lines.)

(Reminder: Watch for *different* time signatures.)

(Reminder: Write in the counting numbers *directly below* the note or rest to which they apply.)

**RHYTHM DRILL:** When finished, *count aloud and clap hands* (same as Lesson 22).

# Lesson 28. Time Signature Identification

Name _____  Date _____  Score _____

2/4 ← 2 counts per measure    3/4 ← 3 counts per measure    4/4 ← 4 counts per measure

A QUARTER note gets one count.

**DIRECTIONS:** The measures below have missing *time signatures*. Write in the counting for each measure. Then write in the correct time signature at the beginning of each measure.

(sample)

1    2

(Write in the counting and insert time signatures.)

(Reminder: Write in the counting numbers *directly below* the note or rest to which they apply.)

**RHYTHM DRILL:** When finished, *count aloud and clap hands* (same as Lesson 22).

# Lesson 29.  Rhythm Quiz

Name _____ Date _____ Score _____

**DIRECTIONS:** Match each musical sign with its description by placing the corresponding alphabetical letter on the line beside the description. In a few instances the same letter may be used for more than one answer.

| A | I | _____ Measure with 3 Counts |
|---|---|---|
|   |   | _____ Half Rest |
| B | J | _____ Measure with 4 Counts |
|   |   | _____ Time Signature showing Four Counts per Measure |
| C | K | _____ Quarter Note |
|   |   | _____ Common Time Signature |
| D | L | _____ Whole Rest |
|   |   | _____ Two Eighth Notes |
| E | M | _____ Measure with 2 Counts |
|   |   | _____ Staff |
| F | N | _____ Dotted Half Note |
|   |   | _____ Time Signature showing Three Counts per Measure |
| G | O | _____ Quarter Rest |
|   |   | _____ Half Note |
| H | P | _____ Time Signature showing Two Counts per Measure |
|   |   | _____ Whole Note |

You are now ready to progress to Schaum's RHYTHM WORKBOOK, Level 1